SCHIRMER'S LIBRARY
OF MUSICAL CLASSICS

Vol. 39

FRÉDÉRIC CHOPIN

Album

A Collection of Thirty-Three
Favorite Compositions

For the Piano

G. SCHIRMER, Inc.

DISTRIBUTED BY

HAL•LEONARD®
CORPORATION
7777 W. BLUEMOUND RD. P.O. BOX 13819 MILWAUKEE, WI 53213

CONTENTS

A Laura Harsford

Grande Valse brillante

Revised and fingered by
Rafael Joseffy

F. Chopin. Op. **18**

Vivo

Revised and fingered by
Rafael Joseffy

A Mademoiselle de Thun-Hohenstein

Valse brillante

F. Chopin. Op. 34, No. 1

Vivace

A Madame G. d'Ivry

Valse brillante

Revised and fingered by
Rafael Joseffy

F. Chopin. Op. **34**, No. **2**

Valse

Revised and fingered by
Rafael Joseffy

F. Chopin. Op. 42

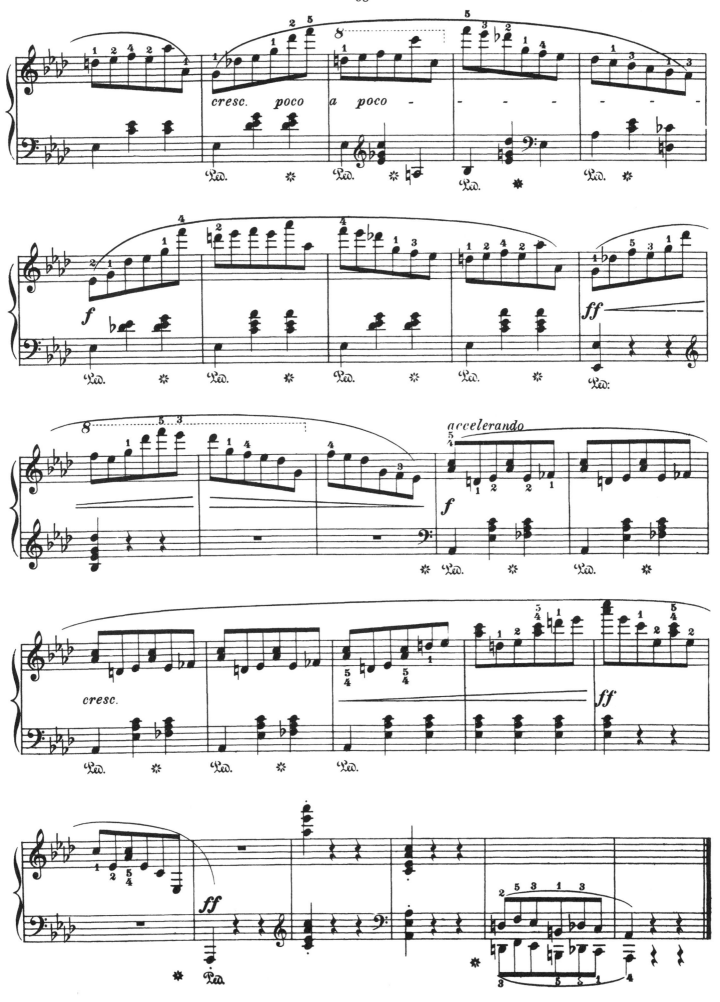

A Madame la Comtesse Delphine Potocka

Valse

Revised and fingered by
Rafael Joseffy

F. Chopin. Op. 64, No. 1

Molto vivace

Revised and fingered by
Rafael Joseffy

A Madame Nathaniel de Rothschild

Valse

F. Chopin. Op. 64, № 2

Tempo giusto

Klindworth:

Valse
(Posthumous)

Revised and fingered by
Rafael Joseffy

F. Chopin

à Monsieur Johns de la Nouvelle-Orléans

Cinq Mazurkas

Revised and fingered by
Rafael Joseffy

F. Chopin. Op. 7, No. 1

Mazurka

Revised and fingered by
Rafael Joseffy

F. Chopin. Op. 7, No. 2

Vivo, ma non troppo (♩ = 160)

à Mlle la Comtesse Mostowska

Quatre Mazurkas

Revised and fingered by
Rafael Joseffy

F. Chopin. Op. 33, No. 1

Mazurka

Revised and fingered by
Rafael Joseffy

F. Chopin. Op. 33, No. 3

Semplice

Mazurka

Revised and fingered by
Rafael Joseffy

F. Chopin. Op. 33, No. 4

Polonaise.

Mr. A. LEO.

Maestoso.

F. CHOPIN, Op. 53.

Polonaise
(Militaire)

à M.ⁱ J. FONTANA.

F. CHOPIN. Op. 40, № 1.

Allegro con brio.

Polonaise

à Mr. J. DESSAUER.

F. CHOPIN. Op. 26, No 1.

Allegro appassionato.

Polonaise da Capo al Fine.

à Madame Camilla Pleyel

Nocturne

Edited and fingered by
Rafael Joseffy

F. CHOPIN. Op. 9, № 2

Andante (♪ = 132)

à Mr Ferdinand Hiller

Nocturne

Edited and fingered by
Rafael Joseffy

F. Chopin. Op. 15, № 2

à Mr Ferdinand Hiller

Nocturne

Edited and fingered by
Rafael Joseffy

F. Chopin. Op. 15, № 3

à Mme la Comtesse d'Appony

Nocturne

Edited and fingered by
Rafael Joseffy

F. Chopin. Op. 27, № 2

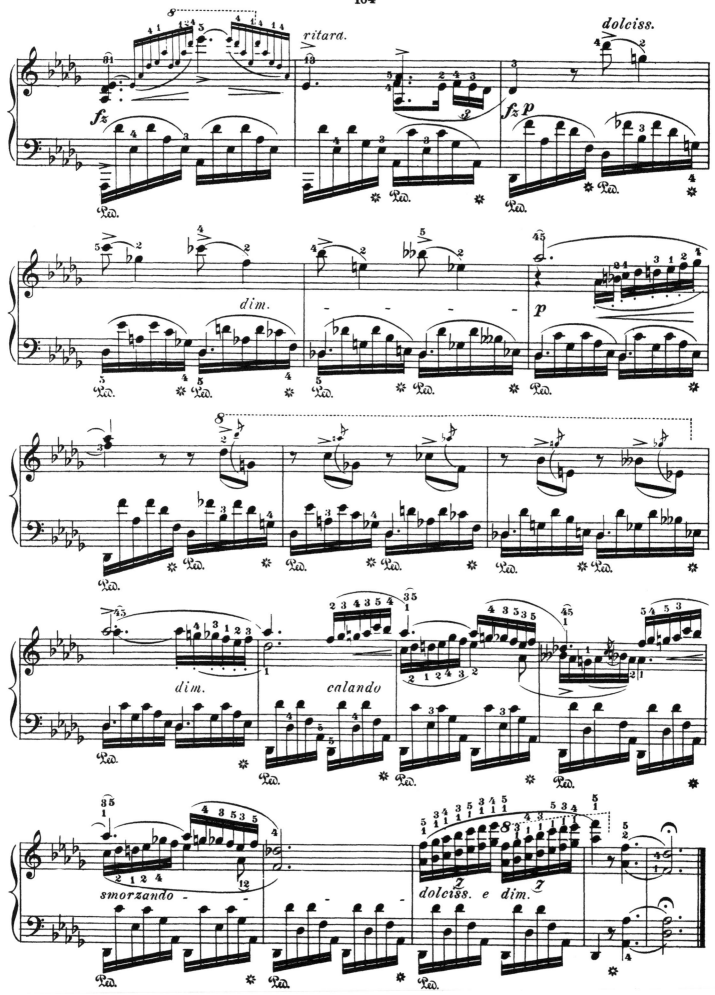

à Mme la Baronne de Billing, née de Courbonne

Nocturne

Edited and fingered by
Rafael Joseffy

F. Chopin. Op. 32, Nº 1

Andante sostenuto

Nocturne

Edited and fingered by
Rafael Joseffy

F. Chopin. Op. 37, № 1

Andante sostenuto

Nocturne

Edited and fingered by
Rafael Joseffy

F. Chopin. Op. 37, № 2

Andantino

*) This measure is omitted in the Klindworth edition

à Mlle de Noailles

Troisième Ballade

Revised, edited and fingered by
Rafael Joseffy

F. Chopin. Op. 47

* In the Kullak Edition:

à Mr. le Baron de Stockhausen

Première Ballade

Revised, edited and fingered by
Rafael Joseffy

F. Chopin. Op. 23

* In some editions:

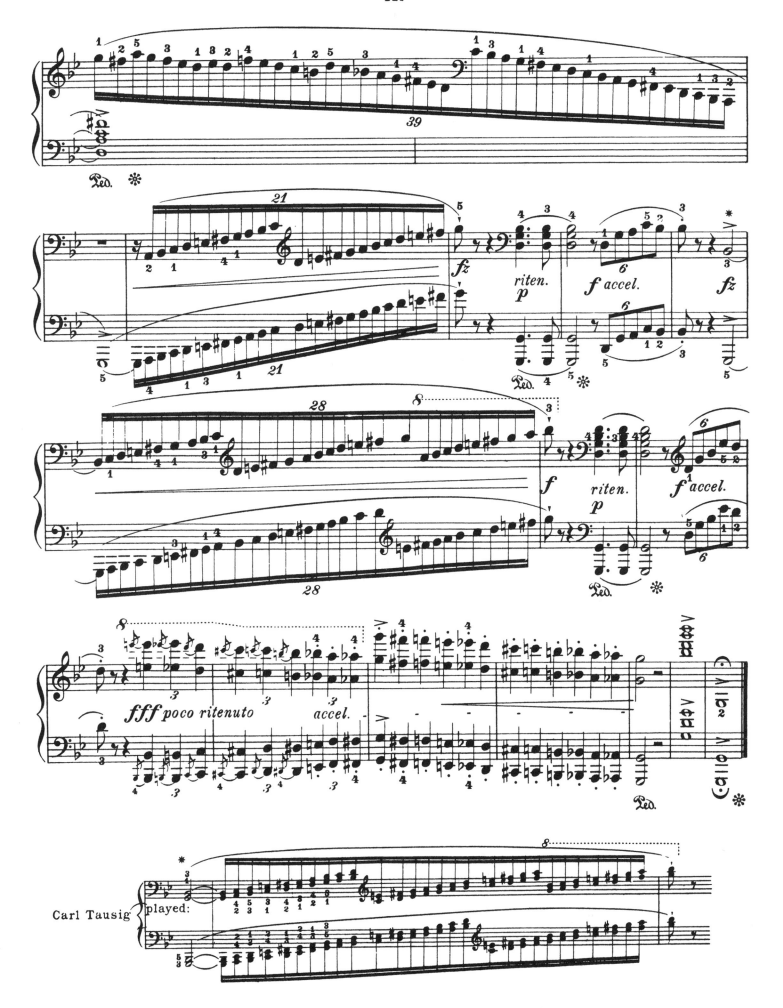

à Mlle la Comtesse de Lobau

Impromptu

Revised, edited and fingered by
Rafael Joseffy

F. Chopin. Op. 29

Allegro assai, quasi presto

Étude

Revised and fingered by
Arthur Friedheim

F. CHOPIN. Op. 25, No. 7

Étude

Revised and fingered by
Arthur Friedheim

Allegro vivace (♩ = 112)

F. CHOPIN. Op. 25, No. 9

à Mme la Comtesse d'Agoult

Douze Études

**Revised and fingered by
Arthur Friedheim**

F. CHOPIN. Op. 25, No. 1

Allegro sostenuto (♩ = 84)

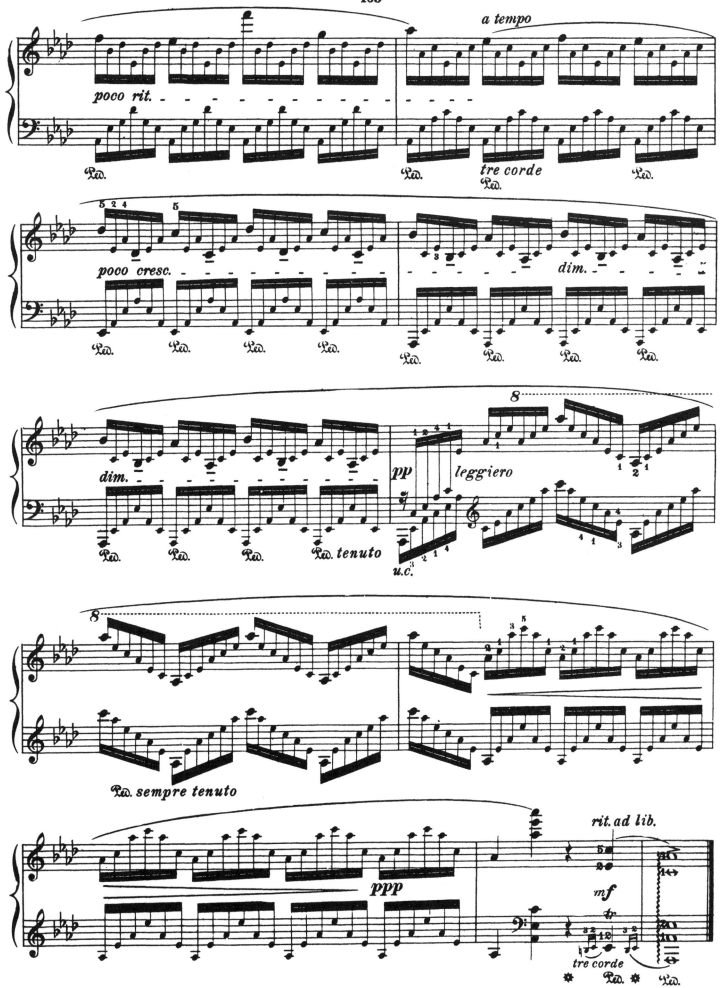

Prélude

Edited and fingered by
Rafael Joseffy

F. Chopin. Op. 28, No. 15

Sostenuto

à Mlle. la Comtesse de Fürstenstein

Scherzo

Edited and fingered by
Rafael Joseffy

F. Chopin. Op. 31

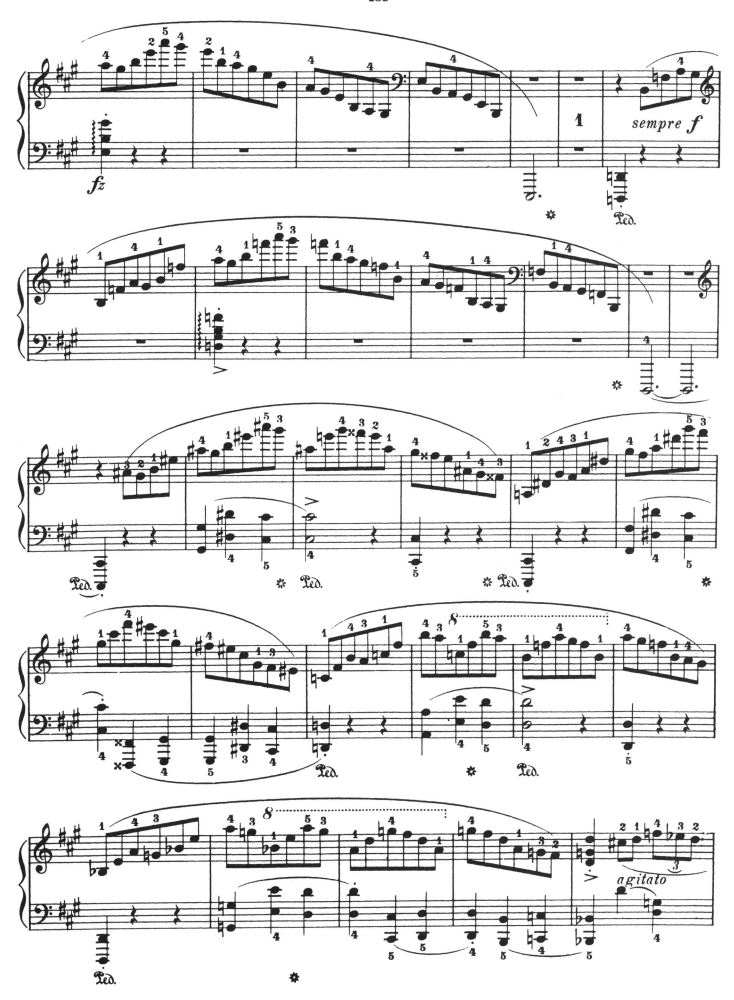

Fantaisie-Impromptu
IV

Revised, edited and fingered by
Rafael Joseffy

F. Chopin. Op. 66

Allegro agitato (Posthumous)

à Mlle Élise Gavard

Berceuse

Revised and fingered by
Rafael Joseffy

F. Chopin. Op. 57

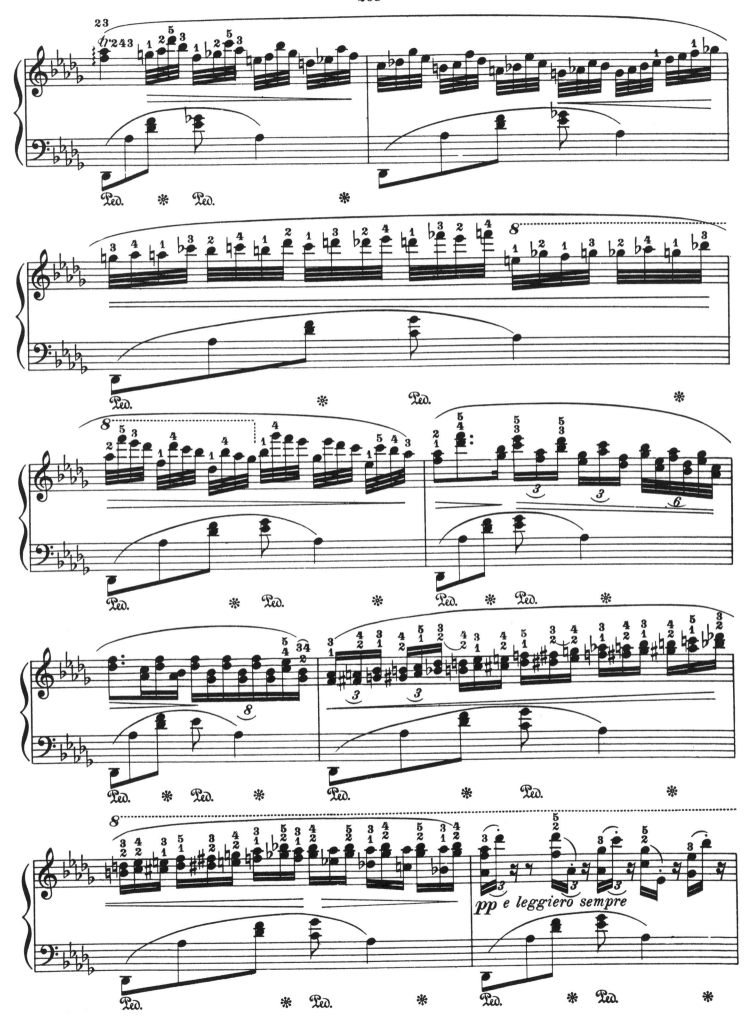

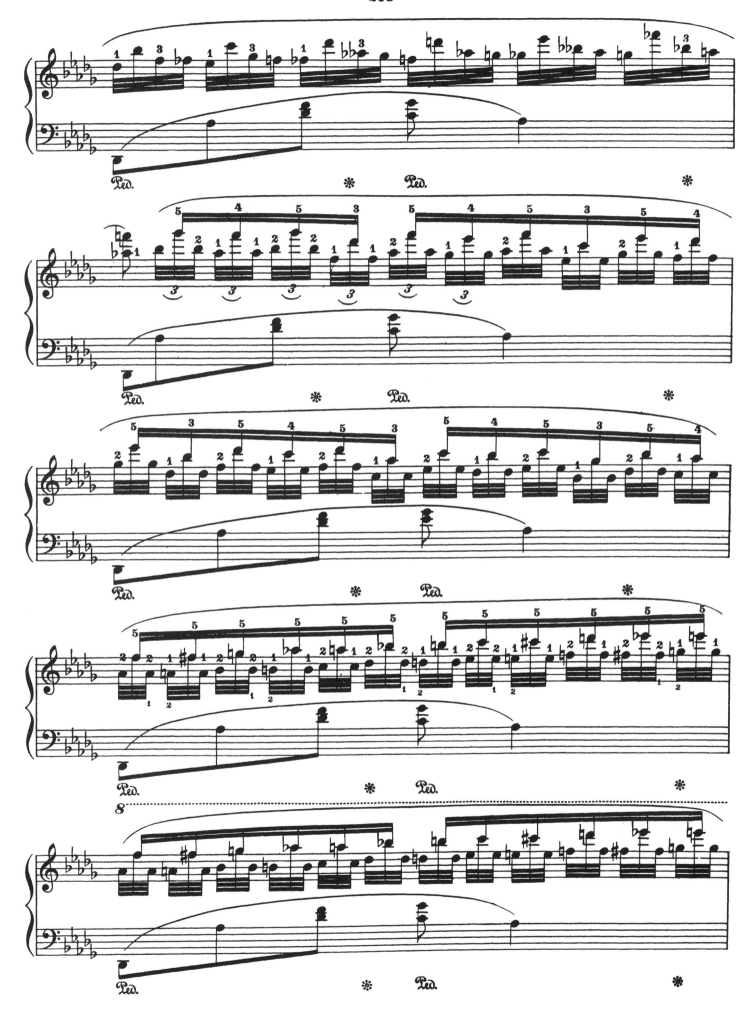

Marche funèbre.

Lento.

F. CHOPIN. Op. 35.